Electricity

Claire Llewellyn

Photography by Ray Moller

W

FRANKLIN WATTS
LONDON•SYDNEY

First published 2003 by Franklin Watts
96 Leonard Street, London EC2A 4XD

Franklin Watts Australia
45-51 Huntley Street
Alexandria, NSW 2015

Series advisor: Gill Matthews, non-fiction literacy
    consultant and Inset trainer
Editor: Rachel Cooke
Series design: Peter Scoulding
Designer: James Marks
Photography: Ray Moller unless otherwise credited

Acknowledgements: Peter Frischmuth/Still Pictures: front cover, 6.
Glen Dimplex UK Ltd: 9t. Nick Hawkes/Ecoscene: 21b.
Tony Page/Ecoscene: 13t, 23tl. Paul Thompson/Ecoscene: 12b.
Thanks to our models: Chloe Chetty, Nicole Davies, Georgia Farrell, Alex Green,
Madison Hanley, Aaron Hibbert, Chetan Johal, Henry Moller, Kane Yoon.

A CIP catalogue record for this book is available from the British Library

ISBN: 0 7496 5164 4

Printed in Malaysia

Contents

We use electricity

Every day we use electricity,

when we
put on a
light...

Make a list
or draw
pictures of
three ways in
which you use
electricity.

a computer...

or a
Walkman.

5

Electric light

Electricity gives us many things.
It gives us light.

▲ *Electric lights help us see in the dark.*

Switch on a torch and look at it. What part of it gives out light?

▲ Headlight

▼ Torch

◀ Lamp

Electric heat

Electricity gives us heat.
It heats our homes,
food and water.

Take care:
some electric
machines get so
hot they could
burn you.

▶ *Electricity
makes us
hot drinks.*

8

► *Electricity heats a room.*

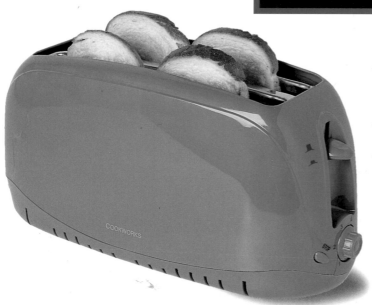

◄ *Electricity cooks bread in a toaster.*

Electric machines

Many machines run on electricity.
They help us do
lots of things.

▶ *This machine
washes the
clothes.*

We plug many machines into the mains. This gives them the electricity they need to work.

◀ *This machine cleans the carpet.*

▶ *This machine dries our hair.*

11

Mains electricity

Mains electricity is made in power stations. It flows into our homes.

▲ *Electricity flows from power stations…*

▲ *along metal wires...*

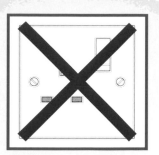

Never touch any part of your home's mains electricity. It is very dangerous.

▶ *and into our homes.*

Batteries

Batteries store electricity.
Machines that run on batteries
are easy to move around.

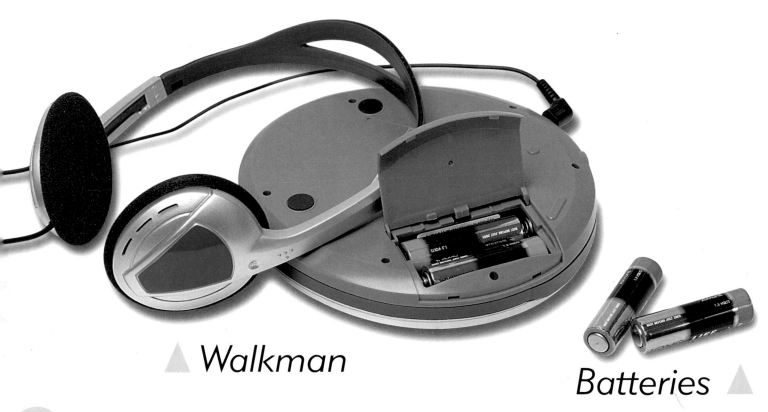

▲ *Walkman*

Batteries ▲

▼ *Radio*

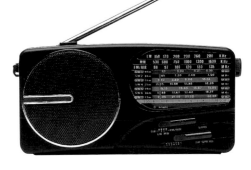

Batteries don't last for ever. Which of these torches needs new ones?

▼ *Hand-held computer game*

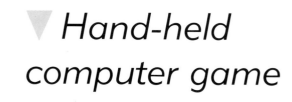

Electric switches

Electricity flows into machines when we switch them on.

◄ *On* ►

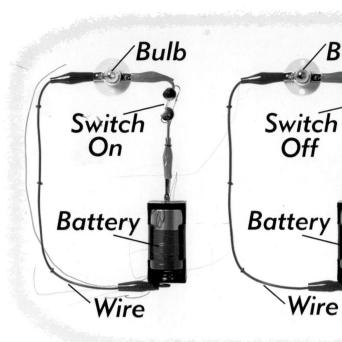

Bulb

Bulb

Switch On

Switch Off

Battery

Battery

Wire

Wire

Electricity flows around in a loop called a circuit. When you turn a switch off, you break the circuit, so the electricity stops flowing and the bulb goes out.

It stops flowing when we switch machines off.

◀ *Off* ▶

The parts of a lamp

Different parts of electric machines have their own special names.

These are the electric parts of a lamp.

Socket ▽

Plug ▷

Flex △

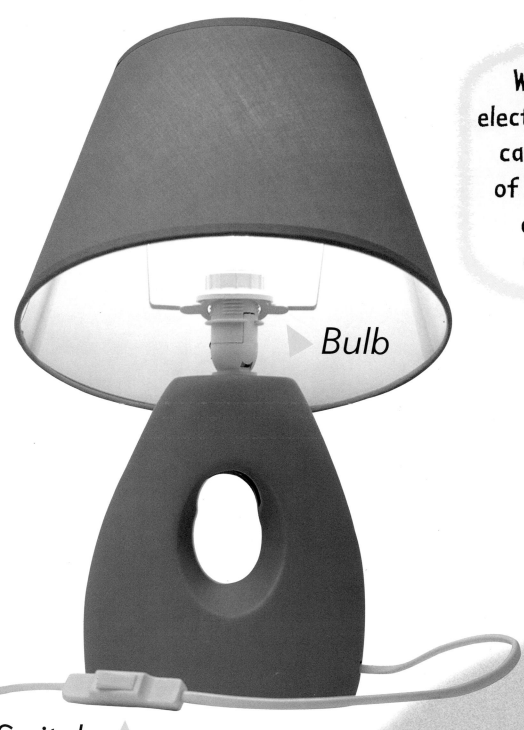

What other electric machines can you think of with a plug, a flex and a switch?

Bulb ▶

Switch ▲

19

Electricity is dangerous

Electricity helps us but it can also hurt us. Mains electricity can even kill us.

▶ *Do not play with plugs, sockets or wires. They are dangerous.*

Electricity and water are dangerous together. A pull cord in the bathroom keeps wet hands away from electric switches.

DANGER

OVERHEAD ELECTRIC POWER LINES

NO FISHING
BEYOND THIS POINT

Do not play near electricity outside.

I know that...

1 We use electricity.

2 Electricity gives light and heat.

3 Many machines run on electricity.

4 Mains electricity is made in power stations.

5 Electricity flows along wires to our homes.

6 Electricity is stored inside batteries.

7 A switch turns electric machines on and off.

8 Electric machines have parts with special names.

 ◀ *Switch*

9 Electricity is dangerous and can kill.

10 I must never play with mains electricity.

Index

About this book

I Know That! is designed to introduce children to the process of gathering information and using reference books, one of the key skills needed to begin more formal learning at school. For this reason, each book's structure reflects the information books children will use later in their learning career – with key information in the main text and additional facts and ideas in the captions. The panels give an opportunity for further activities, ideas or discussions. The contents page and index are helpful reference guides.

The language is carefully chosen to be accessible to children just beginning to read. Illustrations support the text but also give information in their own right; active consideration and discussion of images is another key referencing skill. The main aim of the series is to build confidence – showing children how much they already know and giving them the ability to gather new information for themselves. With this in mind, the *I know that...* section at the end of the book is a simple way for children to revisit what they already know as well as what they have learnt from reading the book.